BRUEGEL AND HIS AGE
IN HUNGARIAN MUSEUMS

BUDAPEST MUSEUM OF FINE ARTS
ESZTERGOM CHRISTIAN MUSEUM

BRUEGEL AND HIS AGE

by Teréz Gerszi

CORVINA PRESS

Translated by

MARI KUTTNA and LILI HALÁPY

Jacket, cover and typography by

LAJOS LENGYEL

Colour plates from the archives of Corvina Press, Budapest

The photographs are by

KÁROLY SZELÉNYI,

except for Plates 1, 20–27 and 32–33, which are the work of

ALFRÉD SCHILLER

© Corvina 1970

Printed in Hungary, 1970

Kossuth Printing House, Budapest

After its characteristic national and almost homogeneous artistic development, lasting from Jan van Eyck to Memling, painting in the Netherlands in the sixteenth century began to acquire an international tone, intricate and contradictory. For a long time, sixteenth-century Netherlandish art was regarded as a period of decline which bridged two great centuries. However, in the past forty or fifty years, research in art history has brought to light a great deal of new material. Furthermore, standards of evaluation have also undergone significant changes. It is now clear that in the sixteenth century, too, excellent and varied artistic successes were achieved and their dismissal cannot be justified.

To a certain extent, it was due to nineteenth-century value-judgements that the art of the Netherlands in the sixteenth century is, in general, not represented as strongly as that of the seventeenth in the collections in the nineteenth century. The Dutch and Flemish painting of the later period suited their taste and aesthetic attitudes much better than the complicated, problematic and mainly Mannerist art of the sixteenth. Thus, in the Esterházy Collection, which later formed the most significant part of old master works in the Museum of Fine Arts in Budapest, there were hardly any sixteenth-century Netherlandish paintings, with the exception of landscapes roughly datable from the turn of the century. The bulk of the material of sixteenth-century Netherlandish paintings in the Museum of Fine Arts came either from later purchases, or from donations. Nor is there a large enough number of such works. Unfortunately, many outstanding masters—such as Jan van Scorel, Frans Floris, Gillis van Coninxloo, Paulus Bril—are completely missing, while the works of Quentin Massys, Hieronymus Bosch, Jan Gossaert or Lucas van Leyden are only represented by copies or by the works of their pupils. The material of this volume was further reduced by the exclusion of the works of some sixteenth-century masters—of Herri met de Bles and of Joos van Cleve—which have been included in another volume of this same series, on early painting in the Netherlands. Also, the pictures of Antonie Blocklandt, Cornelis van Haarlem and Gillis Mostaert are to be found in the volume on Mannerist art. Further, in the process of research for preparing the present volume, some pictures attributed to significant masters had to be left out even though they belong to the sixteenth century, either because they were in a bad state of preservation, or turned out to be copies.

Of course, the remaining material could hardly be described as providing a satisfactory survey of the varied and intricate development of sixteenth-century painting in the Netherlands. For this reason, we are not trying to give even a sketchy picture of the whole subject; it is preferable to confine ourselves to point to those problems of art history which are closely connected with the paintings reproduced in this book. We shall only touch on the questions of the century's stylistic development as far as it is necessary to illuminate the origins and style of works actually included.

Jan Gossaert arrived in Rome in 1508 in the retinue of Duke Philip of Burgundy, being commissioned by his Maecenas to make drawings of antique sculpture. This journey became, as it were, the beginning of the large-scale, close relationship which developed between Italian art and that of the Netherlands in the course of the century. Several artists of the Netherlands had visited Italy earlier in the fifteenth century, but this did not have a basic influence on the artistic development of their native land. By the sixteenth century, a journey to Italy had become virtually compulsory: it was considered a fundamental requirement of proper artistic training and modernity. The influx of foreign art was rendered possible and necessary on the one hand by the attraction of the splendid achievements of the Italian Renaissance and, on the other, by the rigidity which gradually overcame the late Gothic art of the Netherlands. As early as in the 1470s, the first signs of an artistic crisis appeared in the works of the minor Flemish masters. In offering ways out of medieval constraints, of inveterate traditionalism, of an artistic idiom that had grown obsolete and became mere routine, in offering a new artistic approach as well as practice, the example of Italian art was of the greatest importance. The superior power of the Italian Renaissance in its effects on the north was derived from the forms

6

of expression created by the Italians which were of an equally high standard and general validity in philosophy, literature and art. This reflected the social, economic, ideological and cultural transformations that took place in the fifteenth and sixteenth centuries almost everywhere in Europe; and its Italian forms of expression could serve as encouragement and example elsewhere. Thus, by applying in the fine arts a perspective based on mathematics, on the rules of the human body's proportions, and on theories of colour, they achieved artistic results which could be distilled as general principles: thus they brought about the revolutionary transformation of all the fine arts. The Italian Renaissance had reached its zenith around 1508–1509, when Gossaert was staying in Rome. Leonardo had completed the cartoon of his *Battle of Anghiari*, Raphael was working on the frescoes of the Stanzas of the Vatican, and Michelangelo was painting the ceiling of the Sistine Chapel. However, the stupendous achievements of the Italian Renaissance did not exert any particular effect upon Gossaert. The difference between the artistic approach of a Flemish painter, still strongly rooted in the traditions of fifteenth-century late Gothic art and the attitude manifested in the masterpieces of the high Renaissance were so tremendous that it was impossible for the latter to have any fruitful effect on him. Only slowly, and gradually, did Gossaert—like other contemporary masters from the Netherlands—come to understand the scale of Italian Renaissance achievements, particularly through the intermediary of Italian engravings and of Dürer's works, and to make use of them in his art. The elements of Italian Renaissance architecture and ornamentation were the first to appear in works of art in the Netherlands; then, by and by, came the novelty of depicting classical themes; and simultaneously, there were attempts at finding the pictorial solutions of the new spirit. Not until seven years after his sojourn in Rome did the more notable signs of change appear in Jan Gossaert's art, when he started painting small pictures of mythological subjects. In the ducal residences—first Middelburg, then Utrecht—of the celebrated patron, Philip of Burgundy—a cultured humanist, who was in touch with the outstanding humanists of his age, including Erasmus—the prevailing cultural atmosphere was conducive to the introduction of Italian artistic ideals. However, on account of basic differences between Italian and Netherlandish artistic idioms, the realization of new artistic aspirations alien to the northern artistic approach and its late Gothic style—proved an enormous task. The tendency of the Italian Renaissance masters to idealize and to create types and their classical ideal of form was diametrically opposed to the tradition of the Netherlands, stressing individual characteristics, striving to depict details realistically. From the late Middle Ages onwards, the representation of everyday life, of contemporary surroundings, conveying a secular mood, had had a role of increasing importance in the works of Flemish and Dutch masters. While in fifteenth-century Italian art the influence of the sciences made itself strongly felt and Italian artists showed an inclination for theories and a predilection for theoretical questions, the masters of the Netherlands remained empirical and created their compositions not in terms of mathematical perspective, but of visual experience. Similarly the monumental-sculptural approach of the Italians created a basic difference from the pictorial one of Flemish and Dutch artists. Generally speaking, the scope painting was also different in the two cultures: in Italy, the major artistic innovations and their highest achievements emerged in the medium of the mural and, accordingly, the problems of monumental composition and of sweeping forms were predominant. In the Netherlands, easel painting retained its significance even in the sixteenth century, and this medium differs from fresco painting in its very substance and technique. Moreover, easel painting in the Netherlands was closely linked with miniature painting and the small compositions, with their elaboration of minute details, and careful solution of technical points determined both style and studio practice. Even such a few basic differences may help to indicate the grave and multifarious artistic problems to be solved in the confrontation and coordination of Italian and Netherlandish artistic idioms, and may explain why it took a century of experimentation to achieve their harmonious coalescence.

The masters who visited Italy and came under the influence of the artistic ideals of the Italian art were called Romanists, as it was first and foremost Roman art that played a decisive part in the renewal in the Netherlands. This was only natural, as Rome was the destination of the majority of artists, particularly in the first half of the century. In the Eternal City they received the equally strong impact of Roman antiquities, Renaissance masterpieces and the Mannerist works of their contemporaries. They approached the problems of the representation of the human body in terms of Renaissance art—the harmony of proportions, plasticity, the interpretation of movement—by studying and copying the statues and reliefs of antiquity. Some artists who started with the classical authors soon became engrossed in new artistic problems, so that one finds that, in the Netherlands as well as in the south, the artistic aspirations of the Renaissance were closely interwoven with humanism. The influence of Italian art was not felt merely in terms of a passive acceptance. The Netherlandish masters adopted certain forms and structural methods only because their own artistic aspirations did not differ greatly from those of the Italians. Renaissance aspirations represent a comparatively short period in Netherlandish art, and they were not pursued in the same pure spirit as in Italy, since Renaissance ideals of form were difficult to reconcile with the late Gothic traditions of the north. The rapprochement of Italian and Netherlandish art acquired momentum as the new style, Mannerism, began to unfold. During the sixteenth century, Mannerist ideals began to dominate the earlier, strict canons of Renaissance taste, its harmony and sense of balance, both in Italian and Netherlandish art. The anti-classical ideals of Mannerism were suited to the basic peculiarities of Netherlandish art, thus enriching its development with greater effect. This is why the influence of the Italian Mannerists was deeper and more diverse than that of the Renaissance masters. This brief introduction lacks scope to digress into the complicated problems of Netherlandish Mannerism and its Italian associations; but one can sum it up by noting that Italian and Netherlandish art covered roughly the same ground in the sixteenth century. The steadily decreasing difference between the art of the two cultures was in part due to this, and in part to the mutual influence of individual artists from the two countries, which increased further by the end of the sixteenth century. This process reached its zenith in the international Mannerism of the years around 1600.

The social standing, the intellectual and cultural level of painters was favourable in the Netherlands: more like the position of Italian artists than of the Germans, who could seldom rise from the level of artisans. The Netherlandish painters' Guild of St. Luke merged, as early as in 1480, with the Rederijkerkammer of writers and poets, which meant a recognition of painting as a liberal art. Those practising it enjoyed an equal social standing with poets and writers. (The chief purpose of these guilds was to organize large-scale performances, festivals and pageants in which artists, writers and musicians alike had to fulfil some task, in their own field.)

The effect of the Italian Renaissance first made itself felt in the Netherlands in the art of painters working at court, or else at aristocratic residences or in the service of the church dignitaries. It was in the service of Duke Philip of Burgundy that Jan Gossaert made his first experiments in writing the artistic idiom of Italy and the Netherlands. The painter Lambert Lombard, a typical, educated humanist of the period, was, for a time, in the service of the Archbishop of Liège. Joos van Cleve first encountered Italian art at the French court; Bernaert van Orley was the court painter first of the Vice-Reine Margaret and then of Maria, in Brussels. It was here that he developed into a widely accomplished Romanist artist.

Bernaert van Orley became the official court painter in 1518, although he had been commissioned for occasional ducal portraits before that date. Portrait painting was one of the most important tasks of a court painter. Its significance increased as the Habsburg's dynastic policy began to evolve. At this time, their dynastic ambitions to achieve various political alliances through marriage made it fashionable to send portraits as presents to other monarchs. Bernaert van Orley was not a real portrait painter, he was better suited to execute decorative tasks, as is proved by his many excellent designs for tapestries and stained glass. The Budapest *Portrait of Charles V*, with its powerful realism and its bold modelling stands out among his portraits (Plate 1).

Although Italian art exerted its influence in the genre of portraits, it did so to a lesser extent, and did not cause the same crisis as in figurative compositions. It was a fundamental requirement of portrait painting to convey individual characteristics so that the Italian Renaissance trend to generalize and to idealize could not assert itself; only the free Renaissance spirit and its bold pictorial style affected portraiture in the Netherlands, where the changes in portrait painting in the first half of the sixteenth century could be perceived, first of all, in the fresh emphasis on expressing the mentality, the intellectual qualities and the character of the model. The influence of humanist attitudes to human dignity, to the importance of the personality and its freedom of development extended to portraiture. A psychological analysis of the model became its focal task, and although the Italians combined this with heroic conceptions as well as with a decorative, impressive delineation of their model, the painters of the Netherlands attached more importance to objectivity and to rendering the individual characteristics of a face, thus achieving a more intimate realism.

Such circumstances and peculiarities contributed to the development of a flourishing portraiture both in the southern and in the northern principalities. Through the work of Michiel van Coxcie, Jan van Scorel, Lucas van Leyden, Jan Cornelisz Vermeyen, Pieter Pourbus and Maarten van Heemskerck, portrait painting in the Netherlands achieved its international stature.

The first Netherlandish portrait painter to gain international fame was Antonie Mor, a favoured painter at royal courts in Brussels, Madrid and London. His starting point was Jan van Scorel's portraiture, one of the most significant artists of the period, whose powerful, sure touch in characterization, vivid realism and colours affected the development of Netherlandish portrait painting for almost a century. Like his master Jan van Scorel, and faithful to Dutch traditions, Mor retained his objectivity in portraits, trying to penetrate the character and mentality of his models. He did not adhere to the fashionable conventions of portraiture: he chose the format of a painting to suit the social standing, age, character and mentality of his subject, which also influenced the pose and gesture of the figure, the general effect of the colours, and the technique of the picture. He explored with great attention all characteristic features and facial expressions, without ever becoming over-elaborate. He always succeeded in achieving a balance between details and a general pictorial effect (Plate 5). His education as a painter grew more refined under Titian's influence. He proved his amazing

11

artistic flexibility and his personal adaptability by being equally at home among merchants in Antwerp, scholarly humanists in Utrecht, in the rigorous etiquette of the Spanish court, or among the English aristocracy. He could always convey the rank and social status of his subjects, without submitting to those ideas which his contemporaries and the different classes of society had about "beauty", and without idealizing his figures. His incorruptible objectivity renders Mor worthy of being regarded as one of Velasquez's forerunners.

All the portrait painters of the period were more or less influenced by Mor; Nicolaes Neufchatel, employed at one time by the Vice-Reine Mary (like Coxcie and Jan Vermeyen) at her castle at Binche, was also under Mor's influence. But later, Neufchatel, together with several of his compatriots, left his country to escape religious persecution and settled in Nuremberg, where within a short time he became a popular portrait painter among the burghers and scholars. In his paintings, German citizens appeared for the first time showing a proud self-respect equal to the aristocracy (Plates 10 and 11). Neufchatel painted the burghers in their full importance, on half-length or full-length portraits, in the same imposing stance as their noble models were painted by Titian and Mor in royal or ducal courts. The inspiration of Titian and Mor makes itself felt in the muted, elegant colours and in the precise rendering of the textures and the materials of the robes.

After 1530, a harmonious synthesis of the Netherlandish and Italian artistic idioms evolved portrait painting. In other genres, where the contemplative, static observation of phenomena and of nature played a significant part—thus, in addition to portraiture, in landscapes, genre-scenes and still-lifes— the Netherlandish masters maintained their peculiar national characteristics in spite of Italian influences. But the radical differences between the two artistic approaches became apparent in multi-figured compositions, where events, action and movement were to be suggested.

Many of the painters active around the middle of the century were fascinated by the dynamism, expressive power and pathos of Michelangelo's art. The heroic representation of man reached its perfection in his work, and it also combined the problems which primarily interested Netherlandish

12

artists: problems ranging from the proportions of the body, its modelling, the choreography of movement and gestures to the intricacies of conveying emotions and states of mind. The Netherlandish masters admired the works of Michelangelo, but in practice they followed the sculptural-academic, Michelangelesque variant of mid-century Roman Mannerism. The conventions of workshop practice caused the artists of the north to lag further behind the Italians, or appear conservative in comparison, in their figurative compositions. For this reason, they focused their attention on the problems of the human body. Studies of nudes, unusual for northern artists, were substituted by studies and copies from Italian works and antique sculpture. These served as their models, leading to a certain academic constraint and one-sidedness. The situation was aggravated by the increased demand for pictures, so that painters had to strain their artistic resources further and further.

The large-scale social transformation of the period, its religious conflicts, and the struggles for national independence likewise stimulated artistic activity. The demand for pictures, characteristic of all Europe in the sixteenth century, was further augmented in the Netherlands by a rapid economic expansion allied to an enormous intensification of intellectual life. The full-scale industrial development of cities in the southern Netherlands and the fast-growing maritime trade of the northern provinces created a rich bourgeoisie, conscious of its own worth, and this bourgeoisie had an increasing influence on matters of religion, science, politics, and art. One result of their realistic interests in so many directions was the range of their requirements regarding painting, both religious and secular. The scope of artistic subjects was extended and enriched by their strong secular interests, embracing the fables of mythology and history, one of the side-effects of humanist scholarship. In addition to painting, the graphic arts capable of quick reproduction, such as etching and engraving, played their part in meeting these requirements, which reflected a diverse, new, and freer spirit. Many painters of the period practised the graphic arts, mostly they prepared drawings for engravings. In the years following the 1530s, Antwerp became the centre of this large-scale artistic productivity. As Bruges and Brussels decreased in significance, Antwerp took over the leadership of economic life. It grew into the most significant port in Europe, and the centre of overseas trade. The unparalleled economic expansion of the city and the intense intellectual life, rooted in the sundry social, religious and political tensions there, exerted a powerful attraction on artists. About 300 artists lived in Antwerp around 1560. During the wars of independence against Spain, Antwerp was far from the scene of battle and artists found a safe shelter. A market in fine arts was brought into being by the high demand for pictures. Painters seldom worked on commission; they rather worked for the open market; they were not directly restrained by the demands or wishes of patrons: they could create with greater freedom than before. As early as the opening decades of the century, there began lively export trade of pictures, which also contributed to painting becoming organized on practically an industrial scale. The demands of the market also encouraged painters to specialize in certain genres or sets of subjects. Ever since the beginning of the sixteenth century an increasing number of artists came to Antwerp from the northern provinces either for a temporary stay or to settle there. In the course of the century Antwerp grew into one of the main centres where Flemish and Dutch artistic trends converged. This resulted in a reciprocal effect, so that the art of the two nations could no longer be separated in the sixteenth century, especially as a great many of the Dutch masters who stayed on in the northern provinces also travelled to study in Italy, like their Flemish contemporaries. In the artistic development of the Dutch painters Jan van Scorel, Antonie Mor and Maarten van Heemskerck, Italian models played as significant a part as they had done for the Flemish painters, Jan Gossaert, Bernaert van Orley, Nicolaes Neufchatel, Jan van Hemessen or Frans Floris.

The "Michelangelo of Haarlem", Maarten van Heemskerck, was a characteristically Romanist artist of the period between 1530 and 1565. He was an extraordinarily prolific and many-sided painter and graphic artist, whose drawings were mostly engraved in Antwerp. Jan van Scorel had been his starting point as a painter, he had worked as an assistant, collaborator and rival in Scorel's studio. However, his quality as a painter remained inferior to his master. His primary artistic ambition was centred on conveying the plasticity of the human body with anatomic accuracy. For this, he sacrificed the highly developed visual values of earlier Dutch art (Plate 2). He was one of those Dutch Romanists who indulged in theories to the detriment of his intuitive talent. During his three years in Rome he studied the ancient monuments of the city with the scholarly passion of an archaeologist, recording them in exact, objective drawings. One can sense it on his paintings of nudes that he tried to solve the problems of depicting the human body in terms of Graeco-Roman sculpture. The general effect is always abstract and academic: only in a few details is there any evidence of his immediate empirical observations. In most of his compositions, crowded with figures, he pursued Michelangelo's concepts and strove to express grandeur, vigour and pathos; frequently in vain. The individual quality of his work lies primarily in the decorative, ornamental effect of his outlines.

In contrast to Heemskerck's grim determination, the art of Frans Floris reveals his conquest of this artistic crisis. He succeeded best among the Romanists of the period in achieving a harmonious synthesis of Netherlandish and Italian artistic idiom. After studying at Lambert Lombard's academy at Liège, he spent several years in Italy, first in Rome, where he studied mainly Roman sculpture and Michelangelo's and Salviati's work. On his way home, he stayed in Venice, where he came under the decisive influence of Tintoretto. Floris pursued eclecticism, consciously trying to harmonize diverse traditions, those of his own country with those of Italy, with his particular artistic interests. His talent and his artistic flexibility gave vigour and pictorial appeal to his approach to the human form and he also represents a decisive step in the realization of the ideal composition in the Italian spirit. Through the output of his immense studio and the engravings made from his works, his achievements gained universal currency in the Netherlands. Nearly every painter of the next generation came under his influence; as did Bernaert de Ryckere, a less well-known Antwerp master. There is an attractive, signed picture of his in the collection (Plate 19).

One consequence of the increasing independence of intellectual life from ecclesiastical influence was that the events and phenomena of the contemporary world were portrayed with increasing frequency and accuracy. A strong sense of reality, which is a characteristic feature of the Dutch and Flemish people, enriched religious compositions with excellent, secular genre scenes as early as the fifteenth century. In the course of the sixteenth, this trend gained further strength in the work of Hieronymus Bosch, Quentin and Jan Massys and Lucas van Leyden, until by the mid-century Jan van Hemessen, Marinus van Reymerswaele, Pieter Aertsen and the Braunschweig Monogrammist depicted scenes of the story of the calling of Matthew and of the prodigal son set in a contemporary money-changer's shop and an Antwerp brothel. The border-line between religious subjects and genre pictures gradually disappeared, as is shown by the Budapest painting from Vermeyen's circle (Plates 3 and 4). The biblical reference shrinks into insignificance; in fact, it is hardly noticeable in middle distance, as the emphasis has shifted to the group in the foreground, where the group picture points its own moral, in the manner of genre paintings.

This implicit moral likewise refers to the close contact that grew up linking the fine arts to the humanist—particularly Erasmist—literature of the period. The satire in Quentin Massys's paintings of old lovers, hypocrites, usurers and merchants is as sharp as it is in the sarcastically inclined, and mostly satirical early writings of his friend Erasmus. In the beginning of the century genre painting was mostly satirical, moralizing—often aiming at distortion—but by the middle of the century, following tradition and inspired by the encouragement of the Romanist forms, an independent genre painting evolved, in which caricature and didacticism became unimportant.

Jan van Hemessen's works represent a significant stage in this course of development. In spite of their Romanist character, they reveal the half-hidden survival of the Netherlandish tradition of realism. Although Jan van Hemessen laboured to solve the artistic problems posed by the Italian Renaissance, but the strength of his native traditions and his personal sense of reality drew him again and again towards genre-like solutions (Plate 6).

The monumentality, the large-scale shapes and the exalted pathos he tried to attain by following the Italian example are opposed to the characteristic features of genre painting, with its workaday, intimate mood, with the accurate representation of the contemporary *milieu* and with trivial pre-

16

occupations. This discrepancy gave rise to further problems, and to the unresolved duality and hetero-
geneous character of his biblical compositions. However, Jan van Hemessen had qualities as a
painter which make one forget this odd dissonance in his art: the sweeping, plastic shapes of his
figures suggest a genuine strength and greatness, which, coupled with his delicate use of light and
shade, unusual with Romanists, enhances the vivacity of his figures (Plates 7–9).

The young Dutch painter, Pieter Aertsen attached himself to Jan van Hemessen's art, full of problems
but also containing a great deal of initiative. The former worked in Antwerp for a time, where he
became widely popular with his genre pictures of peasant folk. He was the first to use rural figures
as central characters in his compositions without satirizing them. He saw peasants through urban
eyes, as they came to market with their appetizing, fresh wares (Plate 12). However, this did not
move him to paint trivial or humorous scenes but, on the contrary, to create sweeping, monumental
compositions, in which his peasant figures were enlarged to heroic stature. Presumably Aertsen did
not visit Italy, but he was acquainted with the most important achievements of the Italian Renaissance
through the Romanist masters. From Hemessen he learnt how to select his scenes, as well as
monumental conception and the generalizing of his figures. From Frans Floris he acquired the
knack of balanced composition, and the way to enhance the significance of his figures within a
realistic interpretation. None the less, Aertsen transformed these outside influences into his own
individual and vigorous style, with a singular range of colour, with wide, energetic brush-strokes,
suited to his sweeping, monumental artistic approach. He created surface effects in preference to
emphasizing the inner structure of his forms (Plate 13). He was the first still-life painter to paint a
picture (dating from 1551) of the window of a butcher's shop (Uppsala, Universitets Konstsamlinger),
thus creating a new genre. Ever since Jan van Eyck, objects were depicted as still-lifes in various
religious paintings by fifteenth-century masters. But the main source of independent still-lifes was
the genre painting, in which still-lifes were only used to enrich the painting. Aertsen's initiative—a
step of decisive importance—was developed further by Joachim Bueckelaer and Maarten van Cleve.

The first and most important difference between Bueckelaer and his master, Aertsen, was his sense of colour. With his pictures of one or more figures, he followed Aertsen in genre pictures, but differed in giving his figures a more natural pose and bearing, by arranging them in a more lucid spatial composition, and by achieving a fiery depth of colour. He adapted the ideal beauty of the Romanists more than his master did, in his figures, and he made the attempt to form ideal types particularly in his female figures (Plates 14 and 15). In contrast with Aertsen's more ascetic forms, Bueckelaer's, with their nearly Baroque, curving lines, appear far more sensuous. In his early pictures the bright, local colours dominated, but later he took to richer tones and in the painting of his late years the colours grew more tender and light, perhaps influenced by the Venetian masters' use of colour which imbued their pictures with gaiety.

From the monumental and the intimate styles of genre painting, Maarten van Cleve chose the latter. In his multifigured compositions, the figures are smaller and continue their everyday activities with untrammelled ease (Plate 16). In his early pictures, the composition of space and of figures still show Pieter Aertsen's influence. Later he came under Pieter Bruegel's influence, whose peasant genre scenes served as his prototypes in subject-matter, composition, figures and, to a certain extent, his colours (Plate 17). The pale, light colours of his early works became darker and more vigorous under Bruegel's influence. Following in the footsteps of Aertsen and Bueckelaer, he also painted still-lifes which reveal his pleasure in the realistic presentation of surface textures.

The development of the new art forms, the genre scene, the landscape and the still-life as well as the changing, increasingly genre-like approach to religious compositions point to the fact that side by side with the Mannerist movement in sixteenth-century art, realistic trends also continued. However, there were only a few artists who were able to develop a full and diverse approach to realism in the face of prevailing artistic fashions. This needed so great a talent, such courage and independence—to take up the challenge of all the artistic problems of the period—as only Pieter Bruegel had.

The individuality of his unsurpassed genius appears to stand isolated among his Romanist contemporaries. However, on close examination his work turns out to be deeply embedded in the complex artistic problems of his age. He used to be considered an opponent of Romanism, untouched by the effect of Italian art, the only true champion of national traditions. But against this idea which formerly prevailed, recent research shows that he alone among his contemporaries really understood the essence of Italian art, and only he achieved the first great synthesis of southern and northern artistic idioms. Much more perfectly than any Romanist did he assimilate the various foreign influences by using them to achieve his individual and singular artistic aspirations and by blending them organically into his art. But, in contrast to the Romanists, he was not estranged from the traditions of his country. The early, fresh realism of the Van Eyck brothers, Rogier van der Weyden's vigorous and plastic approach to forms, the bold innovations of Hugo van der Goes, the rich inventiveness and the magnificent pictorial qualities of Hieronymus Bosch all had their part in forming his art. Nor did he merely continue along the lines of his great precursors: he transformed them with the sure touch of the fervent revolutionary. The observation of nature had been segregated from the problems of composition in the art of the earlier masters. It was within the framework of traditional schemes of composition that his predecessors tried to present details realistically. In contrast, Bruegel achieved a monumental synthesis of human life and nature, not only in the realism of details. To succeed in this, he needed the new tradition of composition which had been adopted from the Italians. Bruegel's interest embraced all the phenomena and events of the daily world. As a result, he accumulated a great deal of practical experience, which, coupled with a knowledge of the significant philosophies of the period, enabled him to see and present life as a whole.

Bosch's world—still a transcendental one—was dominated by demons and monsters; Bruegel's works display a complete and objective world, operating in accordance with its own laws. His early works point to the completion and secularization of Bosch's art, while his late compositions of peasant life, monumental in their effect, are diametrically opposed in approach to Bosch, the last great master of late Gothic art. He covered an immense distance in one and a half decades: his development embraced practically every major problem of style, from the late Gothic to the Renaissance, and to Mannerism.

Bruegel alone succeeded in tackling every artistic problem that absorbed the interest of the contemporary Romanist masters. With his lively, three-dimensional figures he solved the problems of representing a moving figure with plasticity—the major undertaking of a number of painters from Gossaert to Bernaert van Orley, Lucas van Leyden, Jan van Hemessen and Maarten van Heemskerck, all of whom he surpassed. In his early works he depicted a host of small figures, which covered evenly, like a carpet pattern, the surface of his picture; later, he arranged large figures in well poised groups; in his last period, he achieved a truly monumental recreation of the human figure. A similar striving for the monumental characterized Aertsen's and Bueckelaer's works too, their figures, however, compared to Bruegel's, appear lifeless, as they lack the convincing interpretation of movement, and the connection between figures. Their figures seem isolated and sometimes, particularly in Bueckelaer's paintings, they suggest the atmosphere of a still-life. Bruegel always represented people in physical contact with one another, and engaged in their habitual activities, thus he never isolated his figures from one another, or from their surroundings. Unlike the Romanists, he did not paint figures in conventional patterns of motion: he painted human activities, men at work, or at play. For Bruegel, life itself was incessant activity; and not only human life but of all nature which he did not perceive as a series of static images but as alive, dynamic, imbued with elemental forces.

In his religious paintings the figures—according to the general humanistic trends of sixteenth-century Netherlandish art—appear in the concrete, real environment. It was in Bruegel's art that genre painting acquired its true stature, for he did not depict peasant life as a curiosity, but as a natural, organic form of human existence, with its full complexity of thought, feeling and aspiration. Like Aertsen and Bueckelaer, he centred his art on peasant life, using it to convey universal human significance. He did not either beautify or caricature his figures, but depicted them as they were, objectively, but always with sympathy. He discovered basic human qualities in them, for their way of life had hardly changed at all in the course of centuries. Bruegel was not concerned with the character, the fate or the problems of the individual, or of a single class of society, but with universals: the physical and mental world of mankind. He did not portray personal characteristics, but simplified figures, emphasizing their inner emotional and psychological motives rather than external appearance, perceptible to the senses. In his early multifigured compositions such figures, simplified to basic forms, are almost completely alike, differing only in their clothing and their movements. In his later compositions, a crowd by and by came to be differentiated, and as the figures became larger, their typical features were increasingly emphasized. In his development in composing crowd scenes, and of the individual within the composition, *The Sermon of St. John the Baptist* (Plates 20–27) is of outstanding importance. On the one hand, the crowd appears as a community, closely linked by a common experience; on the other, the delineation of individuals in this crowd is quite exceptionally differentiated. Every single figure contains the artistic problem solved: in every one, even in those with their back to the viewer, Bruegel conveyed by means of varying their bearing, their movements and gestures, the differences between individual responses. His brilliant and artistic interpretation of the complex relationship between the individual and the crowd expresses a fundamental intellectual concern of Bruegel's art: the endless variations of human nature and, at the same time, the common, general features of its most essential qualities. Though perhaps in this late work Bruegel reached an over-differentiated representation of a crowd, according to Charles de Tolnay, his ultimate message is still valid, and could be expressed in Sebastian Franck's words: *"Omnis homo unus homo"*, that is, if we can understand one person, we understand mankind. In this, Bruegel was in agreement with the most consistent humanists of his age.

The environment of the Netherlands, fraught with social, political and religious tensions and a wide range of aspirations, as well as Bruegel's own personality—his many-sided interests, his penchant for philosophy, for reflection—virtually predestined him to express in his works the diverse problems of his age—whether they were philosophical or moral questions, however abstract. Some scholars consider him to have been a Platonist, others—owing to his connection with Coornhert—a Neo-Stoic and libertarian; recent research has discovered his connection with the Anabaptist sect. This offers further proof of how rich in thought his works are, reflecting the widely different intellectual movements of his age. But his compositions are never mere illustrations of philosophical or moral ideas, for he expressed even the most abstract idea in closely observed detail of material things, with the specific means of the painter's art. The more profound intellectual meaning of his works often remains hidden; as is the case of *The Sermon of St. John the Baptist*. At first glance, the spectator will perceive only its traditional, religious subject. However, its treatment differs from its usual representations, for in the framework of the conventional subject the artist re-shaped the composition, adapting it to his individual, original message. Bruegel returned from Italy as a modern artist and a pupil of the Mannerists, who, in representing man and nature, no longer considered the generally accepted traditional or Renaissance standards as obligatory, but who expressed his individual ideas. The social changes of the sixteenth century in the Netherlands—and the new, freer position gained by the artist—contributed to his freedom to work more subjectively than his predecessors; especially as he produced his pictures exclusively for private buyers—merchants, humanist scholars. This freedom in the arts, previously unknown, was another contributing factor in his opportunities to fulfil the innovations dictated by his genius.

His representation of nature is likewise the manifestation of new concepts. Although in *The Sermon of St. John the Baptist* nature has a comparatively small part, it is evident that for Bruegel man and nature were subject to the same laws. The clearing in the woods, its huge trees and the crowd form an indivisible whole. In the lucidly and homogeneously composed space the various figures and motifs appear with matter-of-fact naturalness and, at the same time, they are subject to the strict rules of composition. In depicting man and natural phenomena, he emphasized the essential and characteristic features of reality only, and this resulted in all the motifs—man, plant or object—appearing succinct and significant, contributing to the desired mood. Colours are very important for this evocative effect. In many of his paintings Bruegel used clear and powerful primary colours, which signally enhanced the dynamism and the powerful realism of his pictures. In *The Sermon of St. John the Baptist* the importance of the primary colours is less, but even here he achieved an animated, colourful effect, to convey the inexhaustibly varied nature of life and the countless differences between people. From a distance, the different colours appear as surface patterns of colour, reminiscent at the same time of the primitive painting and of modern art. Thus Bruegel's genius connects the different artistic aspirations of distant centuries. The achievement of the preceding centuries unfolded in his art; and the seeds of many artistic trends realized only in later centuries can be found in his pictures. Bruegel was "discovered" in the twentieth century, the first large-scale scholarly Bruegel monographs were written in the years when modern art was born; this is further proof that even after hundreds of years his art retained its freshness and stimulus. It is no wonder that it captured attention in an age of innovation and of revolutionary change.

By the middle of the seventeenth century, countless copies were made of Bruegel's pictures. The centre of this activity, virtually a craft, was the large workshop run by Pieter Brueghel the Younger. When the great master died, his elder son may have been about five years old, and thus their relationship as master and pupil could only have been indirect, through the paintings in the family's possession. The son's works bear no marks of independent artistic ideas or singular qualities as a painter. To the end of his life, he pursued the task of popularizing his father's works (Plates 28–31). In the workshop Bruegel's pictures were copied, or others painted in his style. There are even some compositions where these two activities became mixed. There are some pictures by Bruegel of widely differing quality existing in countless copies which show that there were painters of quite different degrees of talent and proficiency in the workshop. Needless to say, Bruegel's exceptional talents as a painter were frequently lost in these copies, which were seldom recognized as such by the connoisseurs of generations immediately following his. This is why they did not honour the great painter in Bruegel but rather the entertainer who recorded interesting subjects.

The camp of his direct followers was not large, and it consisted largely of landscape painters. Landscape painting was least affected by the Romanist trend generally characteristic of sixteenth-century Netherlandish painting. Accordingly, it was in this genre that national tradition, with Bruegel as its chief standard bearer, could develop with relative freedom. Among the masters connected with the tradition of Bruegel's landscapes, Jacob and Abel Grimmer, Jacob and Roelandt Savery, Hans Bol and Jan Brueghel the Elder are the most outstanding. It is not so much the œuvre of each of the masters, taken separately, that was significant, but rather the whole of their activity: they preserved and partly developed the results of Flemish realism and thus made a valuable contribution to the emergence of seventeenth-century realistic landscape painting.

In regard to landscape painting, Bruegel's art was likewise of revolutionary importance. Instead of the fantastic landscape compositions of his predecessors, consisting, as it were, of small and isolated mosaic-like parts, he represented actual, living nature, in real space. Though his followers did not understand the revolutionary, novel concepts in his delineation of nature, they tried to adopt some of his motifs, his homogeneous spatial construction and his fidelity to the appearance of the real world.

Some of his followers started from Bruegel's compositions of panorama-like mountain landscapes. One of them, Jan Brueghel, developed this type of picture by painting natural details with painstaking accuracy and intensifying romantic elements. Intimate pictures, representing smaller units of the landscape, became particularly popular among the Flemish painters working in Holland. From the whole which Bruegel proffered in his landscapes they only took particular details as their prototype: the village, the town, the woods, the plain or the sea—and formed each of these subjects into separate pictures. They did not represent nature in its manifold completeness, but only each of its details.

Jacob Grimmer, who was of Bruegel's generation, painted such minor landscapes. In his small, idyllic pictures he depicted the rural scene and the villages around Antwerp. His compositions are simple and compact. He painted with economy and a sparing use of motifs, his pictures radiate an intimate, everyday atmosphere. He strove to achieve homogeneous spatial composition and a homogeneous colour scheme; often enhancing the mood of his paintings by suggesting atmospheric phenomena with delicacy (Plates 32–35).

Gillis van Coninxloo exerted a decisive influence on landscape painters active in the last thirty years of the century. Coninxloo's life was also characteristic of contemporary Flemish masters. He worked in Antwerp until the Spanish occupation, then he fled from the persecution of Protestants and took refuge in Frankenthal, in Germany. Only after ten years did he return to the Netherlands, to Amsterdam, which had gradually acquired the leading role in the fields of economics and politics as well as art by the end of the century. Amsterdam had also become the centre of landscape painting, and due to the presence of Flemish refugees, a great variety of trends in landscape painting were represented, including Hans Bol, David Vinckeboons and, for a time, Roelandt Savery, who were all linked to the Bruegel tradition. Willem van Nieulandt, connected with Paulus Bril's art, was also working in Amsterdam. Under such circumstances, the importance of Coninxloo's move to Amsterdam increased.

Gillis van Coninxloo was one of the chief representatives of Romanism in landscape painting and united the observation of detail, a habit rooted in the Netherlandish tradition, with the ideal landscapes which evolved under the influence of North Italian, particularly Venetian, landscape painters. Gillis van Coninxloo was not the only artist with this aspiration: Lambert Sustris, Pauwels Franck and Lodewyck Toeput, three Netherlandish masters who settled in Venice, worked in a similar spirit. Their paragon was, first of all, Titian, who had created the type of a sweeping landscape, pictorial in effect, subordinating detail to a principal motif. Following in the footsteps of Italian masters, Netherlandish painters did not want to depict bizarre flights of fancy, nor the faithful image of reality, but a harmonious, ideal countryside arranged as harmonious composition.

In Rome, Mathys and Paulus Bril started from similar ideas. In the sublime inspiration of ancient ruins and of the Roman Campagna, they created a classical version of the ideal landscape; their harmonious and well-poised compositions emanate a meditative and idyllic mood. An interesting version of this Netherlandish-Roman landscape painting is represented by Spranger's picture in Budapest (Plate 18). As Flemish artists in Rome were mostly commissioned to paint landscapes, Spranger, a leading figurative painter among the late Mannerists, started as a landscape painter in Italy. His landscape in Budapest is an example of the transition from the early Netherlandish-Roman school of Scorel–Heemskerck–Cock, to the later, ideal-classical style of landscape typified by the Bril brothers.

Willem van Nieulandt, who was in Rome in the early 1600s, was another artist in Paulus Bril's orbit. Throughout his life, his work retained the effects of his master, and of the architectural remains of the Eternal City (Plates 36 and 37). Similarly it was in the circle of Netherlandish masters working in Venice and in Rome—primarily Lodewyck Toeput, Pauwels Franck and Paulus Bril—that Sebastian Vrancx spent his formative years. He achieved contemporary success by depicting soldiers, social events, and brigands, all in landscape settings (Plates 38 and 39).

Within the framework of the ideal landscape, Gillis van Coninxloo contributed the most towards creating the realistic landscape. In the panoramic compositions of this Frankenthal period there are many motifs, decoratively painted, arranged in clearly separated planes of near, middle and far distance. His compositions grew simpler over the years, acquiring spatial unity, and a landscape type emerged with woodland scenes on one side of the picture, balancing a view of distant mountains on the other. Although in these pictures the representation of the leafy trees and the luxuriant vegetation in the foreground is not realistic, they suggest a more intimate relationship with nature and more verisimilitude. Gradually trees became more dominant in his compositions and finally, in his late Amsterdam period, the depth of the forest became his only subject. Though they were dream landscapes, radiating a romantic response to nature, they had a certain amount of verisimilitude to nature. Indeed, these late works surpassed Romanist landscape painting, and from them, seventeenth-century Dutch realistic landscape painting emerged. Several other painters pursued the same course towards the turn of the century, for instance, Jan Brueghel the Elder.

Jan Brueghel's artistic development was not as consistent and logical as Coninxloo's but he was one of the few artists who paved the way to the style of Rubens's landscapes on the one hand and, on the other, to an intimate-realistic style (Plates 40–43). He started from his father's, Pieter Bruegel's achievement, and reverted, even in some late works, to Bruegel's solutions. Then he came under Coninxloo's influence and modelled himself mainly on Coninxloo's panoramic landscapes of the Frankenthal period. He surpassed him in the realistic representation of the details. Brueghel had a singular gift for realistic surface textures. He could convey his delight in vari-coloured living things, natural phenomena and objects. With meticulous care and scrupulous accuracy, he painted the details with the technique of a miniaturist; details which in their total create an idealized picture. Colours played the most important part; in this achievement their freshness and purity, their unnatural brilliance turned, as if by magic, even the meticulously painted details into something beyond reality. But not even he succeeded in dissolving completely the contrast between Flemish naturalism and the idealism of Italian composition. However, this very duality suited the tastes of the aristocracy and the upper reaches of the bourgeoisie, who bought his works: These circles were fond of ideal Italian compositions but, at the same time, enjoyed the realistic details.

Abraham Govaerts followed in the footsteps of the two outstanding masters, Gillis van Coninxloo and Jan Brueghel. Although their motifs, composition and colourism were his starting points, he emphasized romantic and lyrical moods in scenery by deepening his colours and increasing the contrast of light and shade. His handling is not as meticulous as Jan Brueghel's; his brush-strokes are more vigorous and powerful; in painting of vegetation, he attained at times pictorial qualities reminiscent of Rubens (Plates 44–47).

In many respects Roelandt Savery was akin to Jan Brueghel, but more one-sided and conservative

(Plate 48). He was linked to the Bruegel traditions, handed down by Hans Bol and by Jacques Savery, his brother. Having left Flanders, he encountered Coninxloo's work which forms essential part of his art, in Amsterdam. In Prague, where he became Rudolf II's court painter, his style acquired its final form. His trip to the Tyrol, undertaken on the Emperor's orders, was of decisive influence on his art. The austere world of the Alps, with their huge rocks and giant conifers, encouraged him to emphasize fantastic features in scenery. By intensifying forms and colours, Savery created a fantastic fairy-tale world into which he later placed naturalistically painted animals. He too blended the world of reality and of fantasy, with fantasy dominating. With the sharp separation of the near, middle and far distance, his fantastic colours, his forms stylized into decorativeness, his miniaturist technique, Savery still represented a trend which most of his contemporaries had passed by then.

On account of religious persecution and the wars of liberation against Spain, several Netherlandish masters were forced to take refuge abroad towards the end of the century; many were attracted by Italy. Indeed, a whole colony of Netherlandish artists lived in Italy, mainly in Rome; but they also found their way to other important centres of European art; by the end of the century, they had won leading positions and appreciation everywhere. With his works for the Palazzo Vecchio in Florence, Jan van der Straet (Stradanus) rose to an equal rank with contemporary Florentine masters. In Venice, Pauwels Franck and Lodewyck Toeput inspired a pure landscape painting in Italy. More than one Italian painter, who later achieved world fame, studied at Denys Calvaert's academy in Bologna. In Munich, Frederik Sustris became the omnipotent master of court architecture and large-scale decorative commissions; in Prague, Bartholomäus Spranger rose to become the leader of the so-called "Rudolfinus" masters.

But in addition to these outstanding artists, there was a veritable host of Netherlandish painters, sculptors, graphic artists and goldsmiths; in their singular interpretation of Netherlandish Romanism, they conveyed the achievements of Italian art to Europe, and introduced to Italy the aspirations of Northern artists. About 1600 the masters of the Netherlands played a similar part in European art as the Italians had done a hundred years earlier. The Netherlandish masters led the development of international Mannerism, the new style which prevailed in the various royal courts. By the end of the century, pupils grew into masters and they contributed greatly to the process by which the achievements of Italian and Netherlandish art became the common property of all European art.

BIBLIOGRAPHY

The complete catalogue of the Museum of Fine Arts in Budapest gives a detailed history of each work, with a full bibliography: Pigler, A.: *Katalog der Galerie Alter Meister*. I–II. Budapest, 1967. A detailed bibliography of the pictures in the Gallery of the Christian Museum at Esztergom can be found in: Boskovits, M.–Mojzer, M.–Mucsi, A.: *Az esztergomi Keresztény Múzeum Képtára* [The Gallery of the Christian Museum at Esztergom]. Budapest, 1964.

Other important sources:

Friedländer, M. J.: *Von van Eyck bis Bruegel*. Berlin, 1921.

Winkler, F.: *Die altniederländische Malerei*. Berlin, 1924.

Friedländer, M. J.: *Die altniederländische Malerei*. Berlin–Leyden, 1924–1937.

Hoogewerff, G. J.: *De Noord-Nederlandsche Schilder-Kunst*. The Hague, 1937–1947.

Puyvelde, L. van: *La Peinture Flamande à Rome*. Brussels, 1950.

LIST OF PLATES

1 BERNAERT VAN ORLEY
PORTRAIT OF CHARLES V

2 MAARTEN VAN HEEMSKERCK
THE LAMENTATION FOR CHRIST

3 CIRCLE OF JAN CORNELISZ VERMEYEN
THE PRODIGAL SON

4 CIRCLE OF JAN CORNELISZ VERMEYEN
THE PRODIGAL SON (detail)

5 ANTONIE MOR
A KNIGHT OF THE SPANISH ORDER
OF ST. JAMES

6 JAN VAN HEMESSEN
ISAAC BLESSING JACOB

7 JAN VAN HEMESSEN
ST. PAUL AND BARNABAS IN LYSTRA

8 JAN VAN HEMESSEN
CHRIST CARRYING THE CROSS

9 JAN VAN HEMESSEN
CHRIST CARRYING THE CROSS (detail)

10 NICOLAES NEUFCHATEL
PORTRAIT OF HENDRIK PILGRAM

11 NICOLAES NEUFCHATEL
PORTRAIT OF HENDRIK PILGRAM'S WIFE

12 PIETER AERTSEN
MARKET SCENE

13 PIETER AERTSEN
MARKET SCENE (detail)

14 JOACHIM BUECKELAER
MARKET SCENE

15 JOACHIM BUECKELAER
MARKET SCENE (detail)

16 MAARTEN VAN CLEVE
THE REVELLERS

17 MAARTEN VAN CLEVE
PEASANT WEDDING

18 BARTHOLOMÄUS SPRANGER
ST. GEORGE VANQUISHES THE DRAGON

19 BERNAERT DE RYCKERE
DIANA TURNING ACTAEON INTO A STAG

20 PIETER BRUEGEL THE ELDER
THE SERMON OF ST. JOHN THE BAPTIST

21 PIETER BRUEGEL THE ELDER
THE SERMON OF ST. JOHN THE BAPTIST
(detail)

22 PIETER BRUEGEL THE ELDER
THE SERMON OF ST. JOHN THE BAPTIST
(detail)

23 PIETER BRUEGEL THE ELDER
THE SERMON OF ST. JOHN THE BAPTIST
(detail)

24 PIETER BRUEGEL THE ELDER
THE SERMON OF ST. JOHN THE BAPTIST
(detail)

25 PIETER BRUEGEL THE ELDER
THE SERMON OF ST. JOHN THE BAPTIST
(detail)

26 PIETER BRUEGEL THE ELDER
THE SERMON OF ST. JOHN THE BAPTIST
(detail)

27 PIETER BRUEGEL THE ELDER
THE SERMON OF ST. JOHN THE BAPTIST
(detail)

28 PIETER BRUEGHEL THE YOUNGER
THE CRUCIFIXION

29 PIETER BRUEGHEL THE YOUNGER
VILLAGE FAIR

30 PIETER BRUEGHEL THE YOUNGER
VILLAGE FAIR (detail)

31 PIETER BRUEGHEL THE YOUNGER
VILLAGE FAIR (detail)

32 JACOB GRIMMER
SPRING

33 JACOB GRIMMER
SPRING (detail)

34 JACOB GRIMMER
AUTUMN

35 JACOB GRIMMER
WINTER

36 WILLEM VAN NIEULANDT THE YOUNGER
VIEW OF ROME WITH BIBLICAL SCENES

37 WILLEM VAN NIEULANDT THE YOUNGER
VIEW OF ROME WITH BIBLICAL SCENES
(detail)

38 SEBASTIAN VRANCX
JANUARY

39 SEBASTIAN VRANCX
JANUARY (detail)

40 JAN BRUEGHEL THE ELDER
THE FALL

41 JAN BRUEGHEL THE ELDER
THE FALL (detail)

42 JAN BRUEGHEL THE ELDER
AENEAS IN THE UNDERWORLD WITH THE SIBYL

43 JAN BRUEGHEL THE ELDER
AENEAS IN THE UNDERWORLD WITH THE
SIBYL (detail)

44 ABRAHAM GOVAERTS
LANDSCAPE WITH FISHERMEN

45 ABRAHAM GOVAERTS
LANDSCAPE WITH FISHERMEN (detail)

46 ABRAHAM GOVAERTS
MOUNTAIN LANDSCAPE WITH RIVER

47 ABRAHAM GOVAERTS
MOUNTAIN LANDSCAPE WITH RIVER (detail)

48 ROELANDT SAVERY
ROCKY LANDSCAPE

PLATES

BERNAERT VAN ORLEY
Brussels, 1487/88 – Brussels, 1542

PORTRAIT OF CHARLES V

Budapest, Museum of Fine Arts, No. 1335
Oak, 71.5 × 51.5 cm
From the London collection of Ollingworth–Magniac. Purchased in 1894 from the Bourgeois Brothers in Cologne

This striking, monumental portrait may date from the end of the 1510s. Charles V, Emperor of the Holy Roman Empire in 1519, sat for Bernaert van Orley at some earlier date, but only workshop copies survived of that earlier likeness to give some idea of it (Paris, Louvre; Naples, Museo di Capodimonte; Paris, Louvre, Schlichting Collection). Although the Budapest picture resembles the earlier variant, the facial expression and the bearing are different. The determined stance, the proud movement of the head and the sharply-drawn chin express a commanding, superior monarch. The motion of the head and the slight turn of the body to the right convey movement and enhance the vivacity of the figure. Attention is focused on the face: this is achieved by the painter's masterly, truncated composition. From either side of the figure, and from the hat, part is missing; thus the face itself is emphasized even more to achieve its monumental effect. The foreshortened hand placed on the ledge does not play a part in the characterization; it is meant rather to enrich the pictorial-decorative effect.

The truncated portrait, the pose of the figure, the smooth handling of surface texture and, last but not least, the realistic representation, devoid of flattery, indicate Flemish traditions. The Italian effect makes itself felt in the grand outline of the face as well as in the well-poised, tectonic arrangement of dark and light surfaces. Bernaert van Orley did not disguise the defects of the bony, unpleasant face; he rather stressed them with the unflattering angle. The qualities of the picture are graphic in their character, the pictorial solution being rather dry. Indeed, graphic elements predominate in the picture and the forms outlined with sharp contours are only filled in with pigments.

2

MAARTEN VAN HEEMSKERCK
Heemskerck, 1498 – Haarlem, 1574

THE LAMENTATION FOR CHRIST

Budapest, Museum of Fine Arts, No. 4936
Oak, 78.5 × 67.5 cm
The picture came from Britain. It was donated to the Museum by Marcell Nemes in 1916

The painting may date from the early 1540s, that is, six or seven years after Heemskerck's stay in Italy. Michelangelo's influence makes itself felt primarily in the delineation of figures and in a striving for monumentality and plasticity. Heemskerck painted large figures on a relatively small tablet and intensified the crowded feeling by a blue, neutral background. The four lamenting figures are virtually compressed into the confined area, which is defined only by the diagonally placed body of Christ.

However much Heemskerck tried to represent his figures in the spirit of the idealizing, typifying Italian Renaissance artistic idiom, in his treatment of details, naturalistic features rooted in direct observation keep reappearing, such as the bony, veined legs or the stringy arms. The light, bright colours and restless, billowing outlines reveal the influence of Italian Mannerism. This general effect of restlessness is enhanced by the arrangement of the sharp folds of the ornamental draperies. The overhead light gives the smoothly painted surfaces an almost metallic appearance.

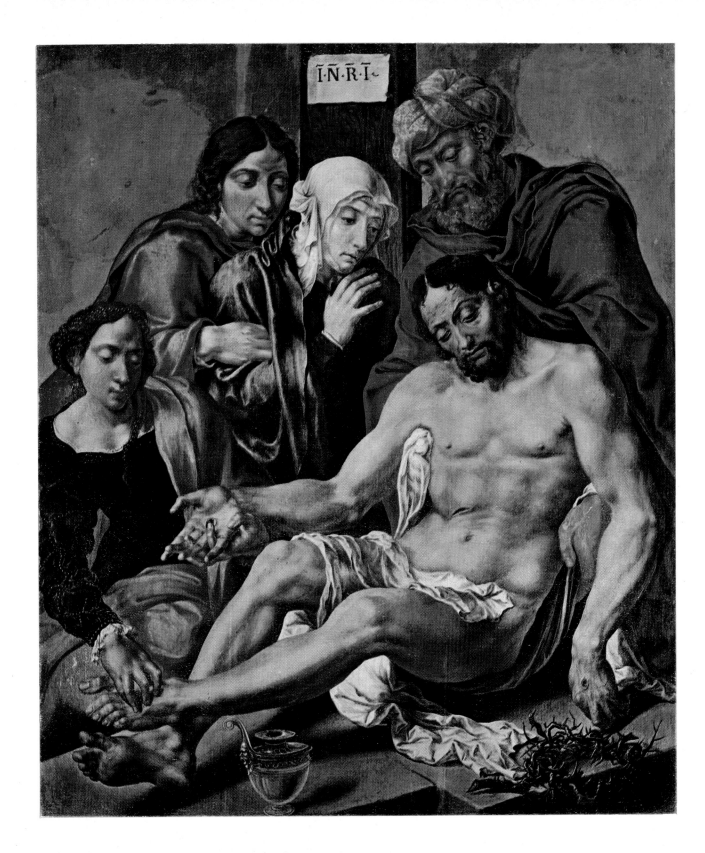

3

CIRCLE OF JAN CORNELISZ VERMEYEN
Beverwyck, *c.* 1500 – Brussels, 1559

THE PRODIGAL SON

Budapest, Museum of Fine Arts, No. 4044
Oak, 84 × 127.3 cm
This painting came from Gusztáv Gerhardt's collection in Budapest, auctioned in 1911 by R. Lepke in Berlin
(No. 49)

A version of this picture is at the Musée Carnavalet in Paris, but different in its brighter colouring. The background of the painting, a townscape, although it is unfinished, shows a view of Paris with the Seine and Notre-Dame. The three iconographical types in this picture were not painted independently but in thematical interdependence. The rhythmically grouped figures arranged in the foreground follow the composition usual in depicting groups of musicians. The scene in the middle where the impoverished prodigal son is thrown out from a brothel illustrates the biblical parable; thus the musicians can also be interpreted as the boon companions of the prodigal son. Five of the figures represent the five senses: the man on the left, touch, the woman with the apple, taste, the one playing the flute from notes representing sight, the man listening to her, hearing, and finally, the woman on the right with the flower in her hand, the sense of smell. This triple meaning, with the three interpretations closely linked, accords with the moralizing-allegorical aspirations of contemporary Netherlandish art. The representation hints at the connection between the licentious, wanton life and human nature, symbolized by the senses which are governed by pleasures.

4

CIRCLE OF JAN CORNELISZ VERMEYEN

THE PRODIGAL SON (detail)

The vividness of the composition is intensified varying the posing of the figures, particularly their expressive gestures. The manner of the painting is sweeping, plastic. In the dominantly yellowish-brown tones, the plasticity of form is emphasized by brown shadows, with fine transitions which can be observed on the necks and heads of the figures. There are many brilliantly painted details: particularly attractive are the different objects naturalistically represented, which indicate that the emergence of still-lifes as an independent art form was at hand.

5

ANTONIE MOR
Utrecht, *c.* 1517 – Antwerp, 1576–77

A Knight of the Spanish Order of St. James

Budapest, Museum of Fine Arts, No. 2532
Oak, 44×35 cm
Dated on the upper right: 1558
From the collection of Baron Pál Luzsénszky. The picture found its way to the Museum from the collection of Ignác Péteri (Pfeffer) in 1904
A variant of the picture is in the Prado in Madrid as the work of Sanchez Coello (No. 1143)

The sitter may have been a distinguished Spanish personage, probably Antonio Perez, secretary to Philip II, or Francisco Herrera y Saevedra, a Knight of the Order of St. James. It is usually mentioned as a doubtful attribution to Mor, although the quality of this portrait is no weaker than most of the master's works. The tension and the spiritual elegance radiating from the face and the eyes point to Mor, as does the objective delineation of details, characteristic of Mor. Although the fine, regular face is moulded softly the difference between the fleshy and bony parts of the plasticity of the modelling is easily perceptible. The sparse beard and moustache are painted hair by hair, with straight, characteristic strokes of the brush. The elegant, distinguished choice of colours shows Titian's influence and is in complete harmony with Mor's subtle taste as a painter. The figure is set against a dark-green, neutral background, wearing a doublet striped in black and green, a shade darker than the background. The brilliantly painted gold buttons and the large red fleur-de-lys look exquisitely decorative against the dark cloth.

6

JAN VAN HEMESSEN
Hemishem (nr. Antwerp), *c.* 1500 – Haarlem, 1575

Isaac Blessing Jacob

Budapest, Museum of Fine Arts, No. 1049
Oak, 119 × 163 cm
Donated by Franz Kleinberger (Paris) in 1896
A replica of the picture is in the Alte Pinakothek in Munich (No. 170)

The biblical scene is set right in the foreground, in a narrow space, with the pyramid-shaped composition of the three figures almost covering the entire picture. Jan van Hemessen painted the aged Isaac as a muscular and energetic figure, whose almost aggressive posture, as he bends forward, does not seem to be a gesture of blessing, but rather a passionate outbreak. The suggestion of internal tension and the dynamic buoyance of the monumental figures point to Michelangelo's indirect influence. The heroic pathos imbuing the figures and the sober petit-bourgeois atmosphere of the surroundings are in a peculiar contrast. The painter did not try to recreate the biblical mood, but he painted his figures in an interior of his own time. His attention focused on specifically pictorial problems: on symmetrical composition, on the plasticity of the foreshortened figures, and on conveying expressive movements and gestures. In his figures the influence of the heroic Italian Renaissance prototypes makes itself felt, combined with the realism based on observation, traditional in Netherlandish workshop practice. The vigorously applied, strong and varied colours give the picture an overall effect of restlessness, which is fascinating at the same time. The landscape on the left is quite separated from the figural composition, appearing as a picture within the picture, an effect achieved not only by the different, light colours but also by the soft treatment of the mountain scenery, kept to different shades of green, with blurred outlines and opalescent colours, veiled by a light mist.

7

JAN VAN HEMESSEN

ST. PAUL AND BARNABAS IN LYSTRA

Budapest, Museum of Fine Arts, No. 4315
Oak, 59.5 × 85.7 cm
Bequest of Count János Pálffy, Pozsony (Bratislava)

The scenes depicted are from the 14th chapter of the Acts of the Apostles. In the foreground, the healing of the cripple is shown; while in the middle distance preparations are being made for the sacrifice in honour of the Apostles (believed by the people to be the gods Jupiter and Mercury). Refusing the crown offered to him, St. Paul speaks to the people and Barnabas is leaving his clothes on his grief. In the background the stoning of the Apostles is shown at the city gates.

The scenes in the near, middle and far distance appear to be independent from one another. The painter tried to achieve unity for his picture by a greenish-yellow colour scheme. This is the only known painting by Jan van Hemessen in which an overall scheme moderates the strength of the colours. However, in spite of the almost monotonous colours, the composition acquires an extraordinary dynamism from the animated movements and gestures of the figures strongly modelled by an interplay of light and shade. The varied range of expressive gestures were obviously the artist's central preoccupation.

Architectural elements also play an important role, serving at once a decorative purpose and also separating the three planes of the composition. Although the part of the building to be seen in the left is made up of classical features, it is anti-classical in its effect on account of its unbalanced structure. However, the townscape in the background consists of lucid and simple architectural elements: solid, prismatic towers and buildings simplified to practically Cubist basic shapes in two-dimensional alignments. The background is enclosed in a soft brownish-green mountain range.

8

JAN VAN HEMESSEN

CHRIST CARRYING THE CROSS

Esztergom, Christian Museum, No. 55.332
Wood, 111 cm × 97.5 cm
Signed at bottom left: "1553 Johannes de Hemessen pingebat"
Purchased in 1874 from art dealer G. Bayer in Vienna by Archbishop Simor
Similar compositions by Jan van Hemessen are known to be in the Soestdijk palace of the Dutch Royal Family, in the Diözesan Museum, Vienna and the Oberösterreichisches Landesmuseum, Linz

This late painting belongs to the artist's most outstanding works. It may have been one of the pictures that influenced Aertsen in his paintings of single peasant figures. The impressive, monumental figure of Christ fills almost the whole composition. A powerful application of light and shade gives plasticity to the figure, which is rendered even more powerful by the dark colours. The subordinate figures crowded together and partly obscuring each other convey the atmosphere of the crowd scene to perfection. As the crowding is justified by the theme, it does not disturb. Against the idealized figure of Christ, the representation of the tormentors, their faces distorted with hatred and scorn, shows evidence of direct observation, though also pointing to the influence of Quentin Massys's grotesque figures. The overpowering effect of the picture is created largely by the strong contrast of cold and warm colours.

9

JAN VAN HEMESSEN

CHRIST CARRYING THE CROSS (detail)

NICOLAES NEUFCHATEL
Mons, *c.* 1527 – Nuremberg, 1590

PORTRAIT OF HENDRIK PILGRAM

Budapest, Museum of Fine Arts, No. 346
Canvas, 180.5 × 94 cm
Inscribed at bottom left: "ANNO · DOMINI · 1561 · — AETATIS · SVAE 28"
From the Esterházy Collection

It was at the peak of his artistic activity, at the beginning of his Nuremberg period, that Neufchatel painted the portraits of the young Nuremberg patrician and his wife. He painted both of them in full-length portraits which ensured a certain impressiveness. The elegant bearing and gesture, the restrained, ceremonial colour harmony of the black costume, with flashes of white here and there against the grey background, contribute to the impressive effect. There is an airiness conveyed by the foreshortened perspective of the brick floor and by the shadow cast behind the figure. The supple silhouette against the neutral-coloured wall in the background not only emphasizes the agility of the figure, full of life, but also enriches the decorative quality of the picture. Although Neufchatel did not come up to Mor in the psychological characterization of his models, with the determined expression, his objective delineation of the face and hands, and the splendidly realistic texture of the clothes, he surpassed the period's average portrait painters.

NICOLAES NEUFCHATEL

PORTRAIT OF HENDRIK PILGRAM'S WIFE

Budapest, Museum of Fine Arts, No. 348
Canvas, 180 × 94 cm
Inscribed at the bottom left: "ANNO · DOMINI · 1561 · AETATIS · SVAE · 17"
From the Esterházy Collection

The companion-piece of No. 10. Compared to the easy elegance of the worldly husband, the wife's portrait shows a shyness and a reticence in accordance with the mores of contemporary society. The simple, compact silhouette of the high-necked, bell-shaped dress, reaching to the brick floor, as well as the symmetrical position of her arms make her appear solemn and rigid. The charming, round face of the young matron, the indifference of her look, turned away from the spectator, and her modestly clasped fleshy hands point to an insignificant personality.

PIETER AERTSEN
Amsterdam, 1508 – Amsterdam, 1575

Market Scene

Budapest, Museum of Fine Arts, No. 1337
Oak, 170 × 82.8 cm
On the edge of the shirt, on the man's breast there is a trident-like emblem by way of a signature. Dated on the stone in bottom left corner: 1561
Purchased in 1894 from the Bourgeois Brothers in Cologne
There is a replica of the picture in the Roselius Collection, Bremen

Aertsen painted several pictures of this kind in the 1560s, with one principal central figure (Brussels, Museum voor Schone Kunsten; Genoa, Palazzo Bianco).

The monumental treatment of the figure bears witness to the influence of Italian art which reached the Netherlands through the Romanists: the stance and movement of the old peasant walking carrying his load on his head recalls Raphael's famous female figure carrying water (Rome, Vatican: *The Burning of the Borgo*). The niche-like stone gate finished with an arch stresses the monumentality of the figure even further. The representation of space is not perfect: the placing of the young woman bending forward gracefully is uncertain and the forward step of the man is likewise not quite convincing. However, these shortcomings are compensated by the magnificent, strong old head and by the realistic surface textures of the incidental objects. Indeed, the feel of the various surfaces is conveyed perfectly: the roughness of the coarsely carved, splintery clogs; the hard smoothness of the earthenware pot, the texture of coarse and smooth skin, and the resilience of the canework basket. The broad strokes of the artist's brush harmonize with his monumental conception, which, however, did not hinder him from painting some details with painstaking delicacy.

The powerful effect is based mainly on the warm, harmonizing colour scheme. The reddish-brown clothes of the man blend pleasantly with his steel-grey waistcoat; the vigour of these colours is intensified by the pale blue of the sky and the white of the fleecy clouds behind him.

13   PIETER AERTSEN

Market Scene (detail)

14

JOACHIM BUECKELAER
Antwerp, *c.* 1535 – Antwerp, 1574

MARKET SCENE

Budapest, Museum of Fine Arts, No. 4069
Oak, 113 × 81.5 cm
Signed on the pitcher on the left: "I B"
Donated by Marcell Nemes in 1911
This late work of Bueckelaer's dates from the last years of his life. There are similar paintings (dated 1571) at the Kunsthistorisches Museum, Vienna; and in the former H. Th. Hoeck Collection in Munich, which was sold by auction in 1892 at E. A. Fleischmann, Munich (No. 17)

The composition is a remarkable example of a composition with two figures, adapted from Aertsen. In this work both the emotional and the formal connection of the two figures is more harmonious than in many of his other paintings. Of the two figures, composed in the shape of a pyramid, the woman is the more attractive, displaying a vigorous, sweeping conception and execution, which can be traced back to simple, basic shapes. The vividness of her dark cherry-red dress is emphasized by the dark grey of her apron and the pale grey of her blouse. The morello-cherries in the basket display the same hue of red, which, as a complementary colour of green, deepens the intensity of the different shades of green used for the vegetables. Buckelaer's unsurpassed sureness of touch in rendering textures is particularly evident in the way he painted fruit and vegetables. His fresh and attractive presentation of beans and peas, with their smooth, bulging shells, the rough-skinned cucumbers, the solid, hard turnips, the wrinkled, luscious heads of lettuce and the scaly artichokes surpassed, from the point of view of colour and sometimes even of texture, the vegetable still-lifes painted by Aertsen.

The fresh, light colours show the influence of Venetian masters, particularly in the pictorial rendering of the background. The townscape, seen through a delicate mist, is painted in delicate, light colours; the pale blue of the sky, the yellowish-white of the buildings and the pale green patches of vegetation here and there create a serene and cheerful mood.

15 JOACHIM BUECKELAER

MARKET SCENE (detail)

16

MAARTEN VAN CLEVE
Antwerp, 1527 – Antwerp, 1581

THE REVELLERS

Budapest, Museum of Fine Arts, No. 870
Oak, 42.6 × 53.4 cm
Probably from the imperial collection in Vienna. In 1848 it was transferred from the Buda residence of the
Treasurer of Hungary to the Hungarian National Museum, and from there to the Museum of Fine Arts in 1896

The style of the picture reflects the influence of Pieter Bruegel and its theme that of Hieronymus
Bosch. Pigler has established that the company of revellers seated around the table is in a
close iconographic relationship with a satirical composition by Bosch, which has survived
only in an engraving by Pieter van der Heyden.*
The only difference between the engraving and the Budapest picture is that in the former
friars, nuns and burghers are sitting in a shell and singing from sheets of music while eating
and drinking. Here, peasants are carousing, depicted in a typical genre painting. Instead of
sheets of music, the open book shows different foods and drinks stressing the obviously
satirical intention and perhaps hinting at the intemperance of Catholics. The satire intended
on religion in this composition is attested by an engraving made from this painting by the
Monogrammist J. C. K. around 1620. The back of this engraving has a rhymed text, accusing
Catholics of intemperance. Painting satirical or moral themes in genre form was in accordance
with the new aspirations emerging in the mid-sixteenth century in Netherlandish art, to
express abstract, intellectual contents in as concrete a manner as possible.
The thick-set, coarse figures are caricatured exaggerations of Bruegel's peasant figures. The
bright colours, thinly applied, might be traced to the influence of Frans Floris.

* *Jheronimus Bosch* (Exhibition Catalogue). Hertogenbosch, 1967. No. 99.

17

MAARTEN VAN CLEVE

PEASANT WEDDING

Budapest, Museum of Fine Arts, No. 7560
Oak, 51 × 71 cm
This painting found its way from Illés Csáki's possession to Lukács Enyedi's collection in 1896. It was sold in 1923 by auction at the Ernst Museum (No. 75). The Museum of Fine Arts bought it from Kálmán Pogány in 1939
There are several variants known of this picture. One, dated 1576 and with the signature CM, was in F. Streyck's former collection (Antwerp); another was noted by art dealers in Paris, and attributed with a query to Pieter Brueghel the Younger

This painting shows the influence of similar subjects painted by Pieter Bruegel the Elder, primarily of the *Peasant Wedding* (Vienna, Kunsthistorisches Museum), the *Wedding Dance* (Detroit, Institute of Fine Arts) and *Wedding Procession* (Gloucestershire, Norwich Park, Spencer Churchill Collection). The Budapest painting depicts the final stage of a peasant wedding. In the centre of the composition which shows a rather coarse sense of humour, the bride stands with two older women busying themselves about her; behind her, the bridegroom is offering her a jug of wine; on the left, a priest consecrates the nuptial bed. The darkness of interior lends intimacy to the setting, as do the predominantly reddish-brown colours. The thick-set, clumsy figures are naïve, grotesque versions of Bruegel's figures. Compared to Bruegel's strong primary colours, in this picture the opalescent, mixed colours appear subdued.

18

BARTHOLOMÄUS SPRANGER
Antwerp, 1546 – Prague, 1611

St. George Vanquishes the Dragon

Budapest, Museum of Fine Arts, No. 1339
Oak, 26.7 × 39.5 cm
Purchased in 1894 from the Bourgeois Brothers in Cologne

This picture, painted with fresh, light colours, figured in the collection as Lucas Gassel's work until E. Brockhagen established that it is by Spranger on the basis of recently published Spranger paintings in Karlsruhe.* It had been established earlier that St. George, and the Roman ruins in the background, could be traced to a composition by Giulio Clovio, which has survived in Cornelis Cort's engraving.**

Compared to the two Karlsruhe paintings, the Budapest picture is a clearer, simpler composition, more homogeneous in its spatial arrangement. It shows the airy, open panorama of a river-valley, with only a small part of the view hidden by the Roman ruins. In this picture the influence of Spranger's teacher, Cornelis van Dalem, is less discernible than that of the Netherlandish Romanist painters. The composition with the river-valley, town and mountain ranges recalls Hieronymus Cock's etchings.*** The treatment of the middle distance, different motifs aligned behind one another—especially the pictorial treatment of the strongly illumined townscape—points to the influence of the Scorel traditions. In contrast with the dynamic forms which indicate an inner tension, in the Karlsruhe pictures, in this painting everything is much calmer, more harmonious, more naturalistic, like the landscape background of Spranger's *St. Paul's Conversion*, painted after Giulio Clovio's picture. The latter is dated by Oberhuber towards the end of Spranger's Roman period; this makes it likely that the Budapest painting, which is closely related to it in its more airy, wider arrangement of space and in the pictorial treatment of details, may also date from 1573–74.

* Oberhuber, K.: "Die Landschaft im Frühwerk Bartholomäus Sprangers." *Jahrbuch der Staatlichen Kunstsammlungen in Baden–Württemberg* I (1964), 173.

** Hollstein, F. W. H.: *Dutch and Flemish Etchings, Engravings and Woodcuts cca 1450–1700.* Amsterdam, undated, V. p. 53, No. 130.

*** Hollstein, F. W. H.: *op. cit.* IV, p. 179, No. 14; p. 181, No. 34.

19

BERNAERT DE RYCKERE
Kortrijk, *c.* 1535 – Antwerp, 1590

Diana Turning Actaeon into a Stag

Budapest, Museum of Fine Arts, No. 378
Oak, 48 × 70.5 cm (of this 3 cm were added later at the foot and 2 cm to the right of the tablet)
Signed on the rock on the left: "1582 B. D. Rickere IV."
In 1781 the painting was transferred from the imperial collection in Vienna to the Castle at Pozsony (Bratislava) and from there to the Buda residence of the Treasurer of Hungary. In 1848 it passed into the ownership of the Hungarian National Museum, and from there to the Museum of Fine Arts in 1896

This less well-known artist represented the mythological scene which was so often chosen as a theme of paintings in the spirit of Netherlandish traditions set in a rich landscape. The landscape is the real subject of the picture; the figures appear only as staffage, all the more so as the mythological scene is placed in the lowest section of the composition with the various green shades of the splendid landscape filling in most of the picture's surface area. The dark greens made to appear deeper in combination with the brown shades set off to perfection the plasticity and the pearly, light colours of the nudes modelled with soft, greenish-grey shadows. The facial types—broad at eye-level and narrowing sharply at the chin—resemble those of Frans Floris.

The apparently random selection of the mountain view, with only a few landscape elements, seems natural and familiar. The fact that the foliage of the various trees is not depicted as uniform, not according to pictorial conventions, but with botanical verisimilitude, proves the artist's strong sense of reality.

20

PIETER BRUEGEL THE ELDER
Bruegel, *c.* 1525 – Brussels, 1569

The Sermon of St. John the Baptist

Budapest, Museum of Fine Arts, No. 51.2829
Oak, 95 × 160.5 cm
Signed at bottom right: " · BRVEGEL · M · D · LXVI."
From the Batthyány castle at Nagycsákány
A signed version (or copy?) of this painting is in Vittorio Duca's collection in Milan. There were a great many copies made of this picture, most of them attributed to Pieter Brueghel the Younger

Bruegel transformed here completely the traditional iconography of the subject. By emphasizing its human, everyday relevance, he endowed the traditional subject with fresh life and new meaning. With the figures in contemporary clothes and set in an atmospheric landscape, the picture looks secular, more like a genre painting. The varied, motley crowd, held together by an artistic unity, seems to be the picture's real subject.

Recent investigations show that the picture contains a more profound meaning. The theme, and to a certain extent even its treatment are connected with the Anabaptist movement, whose members always gathered in the open air for divine service.* Bruegel may have been a member of this sect. Their theology was dominated by the belief that the end of the world was near, and with it, the last judgement. Thus the Sermon of St. John, looking like an itinerant preacher in this picture, refers to penitence and to the salvation which awaited those who were baptized once again.

The scene of the sermon is a clearing in the woods, near a city, where a great crowd has gathered. The two thick tree-trunks of the left foreground and the right, as well as the perspective of the crowd convey a sense of space very convincingly. In accordance with the structural principles of the master's late works, the composition is distinctly diagonal: starting from the lower right-hand corner, the crowd spreads across, into the picture. The spacious, airy panorama of the background landscape painted in fresh, light colours is seen from the wood, as if from a window, thus making the woods seem more enclosed and the crowd more dense. Depicting the numerous figures standing or sitting close to one another and partially obscuring one another, thus forming a real crowd scene, was unique in the art of the period.

* Auner, M.: "Pieter Bruegel. Umrisse eines Lebensbildes." *Jahrbuch der Kunsthistorischen Sammlungen in Wien* 52 (1956), pp. 109–118.

The Sermon of St. John the Baptist (detail)

However, on closer observation it appears that the crowd is not homogeneous after all; it consists of groups, large or small, arranged according to a certain rhythm. The ring of people around St. John is more dense, the groups are crammed together more than on the right, where the figures are less closely linked, more colourful and more individually characterized. Every single figure is characterized by a masterly subtle psychological observation without ever giving too much emphasis to their individual features. According to the age, sex, status, education, health and momentary disposition, individual responses to the sermon are shown by characteristic expressions. Thus, on close observation innumerable animated, interesting scenes appear, superbly painted, but these details are not noticeable from a certain distance, as they blend into an overall effect of an anonymous crowd.

Although the congregation of over two hundred lacks scope to depict as rich a variety of movement, no two figures are identical. Bruegel's inexhaustible imagination is displayed in his picture of people standing or sitting in so many poses which are all natural and lively, and convey that each of the postures is momentary, temporary. The vivacity and variety of his compositions stem from this, and these qualities are further enhanced by the vigour of his colours.

The colour scheme of this painting differs to a certain extent from his other late works. On the left, he used grey, green and brown hues blending into a generally dark tone, with faces looking like light, vibrating spots. On the right there is more sunlight, so that pale and mixed colours predominate. Evidently Bruegel took delight in depicting the different costumes of the large figures in the foreground. The mixed yellow, blue and red colours appear particularly delicate and distinguished juxtaposed with dark, muted colours. The contrast of these two different colour schemes on either sides of the composition increases the visual effectiveness of the painting.

THE SERMON OF ST. JOHN THE BAPTIST (detail)

Wearing red, baggy trousers, a moustached man with high cheekbones is standing at the tree on the left, looking out of the picture. According to M. Auner, it is the portrait of Count Boldizsár Batthyány. The painting was in the possession of the Batthyány family for several centuries and Auner postulated that the figure—the Hungarian facial type and dress—represents the Hungarian aristocrat who commissioned the picture. He kept in touch with famous humanists and scholars; on one occasion he invited the botanist Clusius, who was also a Lutheran, to his castle. The latter was a friend of Johannes Sambucus, who was in turn a friend of Ortelius, the renowned geographer, and of Plantin, the famous printer and publisher. The latter both belonged to the circle of Bruegel's friends. According to Auner it is possible that Batthyány's commission for the picture was transmitted by Sambucus to Bruegel in the Netherlands.

Against this theory one can quote an inventory of the property left by Governor Albrecht, dated 1639, which lists a Bruegel painting of *The Sermon of St. John the Baptist*, with measurements roughly similar to those of the Budapest painting. Also, it is difficult to explain how there could have been so many copies made in the late sixteenth and early seventeenth centuries of a painting that was sent to Hungary, to the Batthyány family, as early as 1569–70. In accepting Auner's theory, one must also assume that there was either another version by Bruegel, or an early copy, from which others were then copied. Until further evidence comes to light, the question must remain open.

The Sermon of St. John the Baptist (detail)

The preaching Saint is a thin, ascetic, ethereal figure. His left hand points at Christ, the future Saviour, who is clothed in blue. Bruegel represented Christ simply, like another member of the congregation. No one in the crowd looks at Him, His inclusion in the composition is symbolic: the preacher is speaking of Him. He is, as it were, a pictorial incarnation of the preacher's words.

A tight group of bearded figures, clothed like the Baptist, stand behind him; presumably the preacher is one of them, the Elders of the sect. Their faces reflect severity, self-confidence and keen attention.

THE SERMON OF ST. JOHN THE BAPTIST (detail)

The figures represented on the upper right are distinctly segregated from the crowd. According to Auner, they are the so-called chosen ones, models to encourage the others. Auner also supposes that the young woman in the red dress is Bruegel's wife and the older one, wearing grey, is his mother-in-law. He considers the profile of the bearded man to be Bruegel's self-portrait.

PIETER BRUEGEL THE ELDER

The Sermon of St. John the Baptist (detail)

Even the comparatively less involved group, those sitting right in front of the preacher, is admirably modulated. One of the men is listening to the Baptist's words with closed eyes, his round-headed companion sitting behind him shows the effort required not to miss a single word of the sermon. With a daydreaming expression on her face, a woman in red leans comfortably against a tree-trunk, listening. In the centre of the crowd, somebody is seen taken ill; with his mouth open, he is gasping for air. An elderly neighbour is holding him up while still watching the preacher and listening to his words.

PIETER BRUEGEL THE ELDER

THE SERMON OF ST. JOHN THE BAPTIST (detail)

To the right, the exotic figures in picturesque costumes in the foreground are not merely creations of the painter's fancy: they are characters taken from the life of a large Flemish city. Businessmen, sailors, financiers gathered in Antwerp in the sixteenth century from every corner of the world, people of all colours, races and nationalities, who stayed for shorter or longer periods. Thus a Chinese woman with her large hat, or a Chinaman with a pigtail must have been an everyday sight in Antwerp.

THE SERMON OF ST. JOHN THE BAPTIST (detail)

Almost in the centre of the foreground an elegant man in black can be seen with a gipsy telling his fortune. From various attempts at identifying the man, who is looking out of the picture, it seems most probable that the distinguished presence is a representative of the hated Spanish authorities. According to Auner, he may be Thomas Armenteros, a Privy Councillor to Margaret of Parma. On some of the seventeenth-century copies this figure cannot be found. After the conclusion of the peace treaty with Spain which established the Southern Netherlands as continuing under Spanish sway, artists were afraid to expose a well-known Spanish personage to obloquy, as fortune-telling by a gipsy was considered as godlessness. In this sense, the gentleman in black represented godlessness contrasted with the faithful listeners.

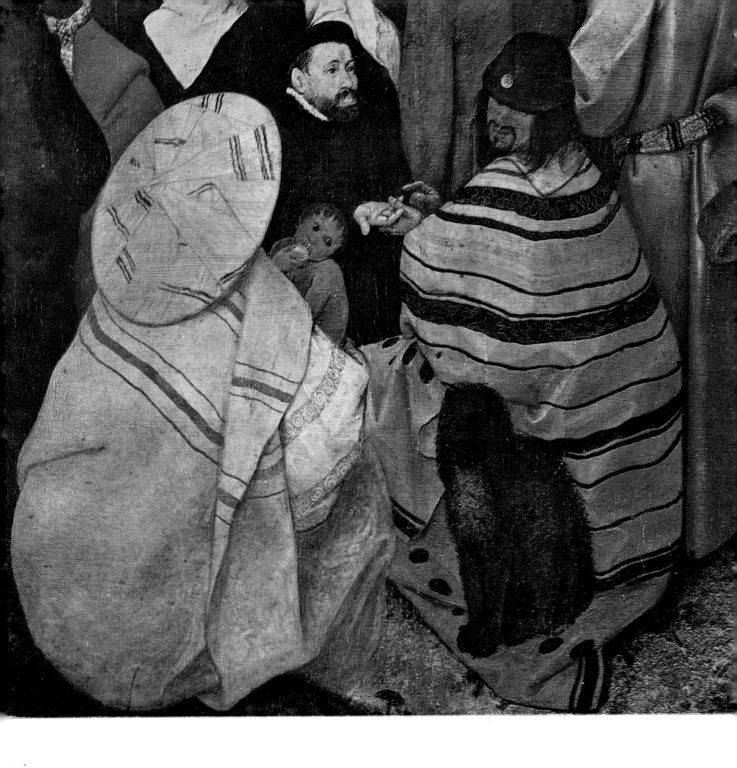

28

PIETER BRUEGHEL THE YOUNGER
Brussels, 1564 – Antwerp, 1637–38

The Crucifixion

Budapest, Museum of Fine Arts, No. 1038
Oak, 82 × 123 cm
Signed at bottom left: "P · BREVGHEL · 1617"
Purchased in 1891 from Th. van Heemstede Obel (Amsterdam)
There are several versions of this painting, all known to be the works of the master, the best being in the Brussels collection of Mme J. van Gysel

Several views have been propounded by experts about the origins of this composition: some think it is a copy of a lost original by Pieter Bruegel the Elder (A. L. Romdahl, G. Hulin de Loo, L. van Puyvelde), others take it to be the entirely original work of the younger Brueghel (G. Glück), while another recent opinion holds that it might be traced to a painting by Bosch (Charles de Tolnay).

Whereas on the different exemplars the part with figures is almost completely identical, the scenic backgrounds vary from one another. This bears out the assumption that it is a copy of another master's work. Usually copyists allowed themselves greater independence in painting the parts representing landscapes and townscapes.

Moreover, in the Budapest picture the treatment of the figures and of the background is strikingly different: while the figures are painted with an archaistic, almost smooth surface, the view of the town in the distance shows a degree of impasto.

There are similar compositions of small groups only loosely connected to form crowd scenes — among Pieter Bruegel the Elder's works, such as *Christ Carrying the Cross* and *The Massacre of the Innocents* (Vienna, Kunsthistorisches Museum). The figure types are also Bruegelesque. We may assume from this that our picture was copied from a lost composition of the great master.

The technique is dry, lacking freshness or spontaneity. Adjusting himself to the general trends of the first decades of the seventeenth century, the master abstained from using strong primary colours and painted the foreground and the middle distance in a greyish brown tone, whereas he painted the background in cold, greenish-blue hues.

29

PIETER BRUEGHEL THE YOUNGER

VILLAGE FAIR

Budapest, Museum of Fine Arts, No. 7613
Oak, 114 x 161 cm
This picture, originating from the collection of A. G. Hoschek van Mühlheim (Prague), was sold by auction at G. Pisko's in Vienna in 1909 (No. 8). Later the painting reappeared in Rome, at Simonetti's, and was purchased by Baron Paul Kuffner, who donated it to the Museum in 1939
Another painting of the artist's, similar in subject and format, is in the Joannaeum, Graz

The recently cleaned Budapest picture is one of the works by Pieter Brueghel the Younger which show his best quality as a painter. The figures are fresher and more animated than in his more average works, and the pictorial treatment of the townscape is likewise very attractive. The composition of the animated village entertainment recalls the structure of Pieter Bruegel the Elder's painting *Children's Games* in Vienna (Kunsthistorisches Museum). The milling crowd depicted in apparent disorder are actually arranged in a strict order of composition, as is the Vienna painting mentioned above, in two diagonal lines intersecting at the centre. By this arrangement, on the one hand, the depth of space is forcibly conveyed and, on the other, the dynamism of the composition is intensified. By the groups along the diagonals becoming denser near the centre, a powerful feeling of movement is created in the foreground and the middle. In contrast, the space in the background, in front of the massive church there, is a quiet, intimate corner: this enhances the bright and vivacious impression of the fair.

30

PIETER BRUEGHEL THE YOUNGER

VILLAGE FAIR (detail)

PIETER BRUEGHEL THE YOUNGER

VILLAGE FAIR (detail)

JACOB GRIMMER
Antwerp, *c.* 1525 – Antwerp, 1590

SPRING

Budapest, Museum of Fine Arts, No. 555
Oak, 35.5 x 60 cm
Donated by László Pyrker in 1836

This series of landscapes representing the four seasons, three of which are shown here, reflects the influence of Bruegel in motifs, composition and in the staffage figures. As usual, Grimmer selects a small section of the countryside, without permitting the eye to roam the distance, enclosing the view by the pleasantly curved and sweepingly painted slope of a hill, thus creating an enclosed, unified space to give an intimate frame to small figures engaged in the labours of the spring. In depicting the various tasks for each season Grimmer followed the centuries-old iconographic conventions. However, spring is no longer indicated merely by the tasks of figures, as was customary in pictures of the seasons, prior to Bruegel, but rather the entire painterly interpretation. The fresh rebirth of nature is suggested by various shades of green which create an attractive harmony with the rosy and greyish colours of the houses within the overall greenish-grey tone. Pale grey clouds hide the sky and thus only a filtered light illuminates the landscape, its characteristic spring mood brought about mainly by this singular lighting.

33 JACOB GRIMMER

Spring (detail)

34

JACOB GRIMMER

AUTUMN

Budapest, Museum of Fine Arts, No. 557
Oak, 36 × 60 cm
Donated by László Pyrker in 1836

To characterize autumn, the painter chose a coastal landscape. Almost half the composition is taken up by the greyness of sky and water, hardly separable from each other, which decides the atmospheric colour of the picture. This side of the coast, the slopes of two hills stretch on either side. On the left wood-cutters work in front of a steep-roofed house. The slender, bare trees and the figures stopping, cramped with cold, convey the feel of frosty windy weather. The sun does not shine on this part of the picture and thus everything is rather dreary and sombre. In the middle distance darkness has nearly closed in on the small cottages nestling under the hill. The parts still lit by sunshine are bright and colourful: the hillside on the right is bathed in reddish-gold tints and the river in front glimmers with metallic blue reflections. The background is brightest, from the light falling on the sea and reflected by it, appearing greyish-white in the misty distance; along the coast, it looks slightly darker, shaded with greenish-brown. The capriciously broken coastline with peninsulas jutting into the water is particularly attractive; the distant townships are painted with almost an impressionistic touch.

35

JACOB GRIMMER

WINTER

Budapest, Museum of Fine Arts, No. 558
Oak, 36.5 × 59.5 cm
Signed at the bottom left: "Grimmer fecit 1575."
Donated by László Pyrker in 1836

Of Grimmer's four pictures in Budapest, this is closest to Bruegel's compositions of similar subjects. Flanked by small houses, the frozen pond with tiny figures skating, walking and chattering on the ice are reminiscent of Bruegel's *Winter Landscape* in Brussels (Delporte Collection) and of the detail on the right of his painting *January* (Vienna, Kunsthistorisches Museum). Like Bruegel, Grimmer too chose a vantage point somewhat above the pond to paint the pleasures of winter, he too emphasized the role of the fascinating arabesques presented by the branches of the bare trees. However, the colour schemes of his paintings differ greatly from his prototype. Even in depicting a wintery world, covered in white, he strove for a colourful effect, almost like the effect of water-colours: the ice is pale greenish-blue, the houses are yellow, light red and shades of pink; blue and yellow tints even suffuse the sky.

36

WILLEM VAN NIEULANDT THE YOUNGER
Antwerp, 1584 – Amsterdam, 1635

VIEW OF ROME WITH BIBLICAL SCENES

Budapest, Museum of Fine Arts, No. 207
Oak, 49.3 × 76 cm
Signed at the bottom right: "GVIL NIÈVLANT · 1628."
The monogramme "NV" is carved into the wood on the reverse side
From the Esterházy Collection

At the exhibition staged by the R. Finck Gallery in 1965 a similar composition of Willem van Nieulandt's was shown.* In its background, as in our picture, a view of Rome is combined with scenes from the story of Jacob (the birth of Benjamin and Rachel's death), likewise arranged in small groups starting from the foreground and proceeding diagonally to the left. In the Budapest picture, the earlier scenes of Jacob's story can be seen. On the right, by the Igel Memorial, Jacob and his family secretly are preparing their journey with camels and loaded mules and with the sheep to be herded away (Genesis 31, 17–18). The two women seated in the foreground are Rachel and Leah talking to their father, who having overtaken the surreptitiously departed group demands that the idols hidden by Rachel should be returned (Genesis 31, 33–35).

This is Nieulandt's last known signed painting, showing that even in his old age, the master continued in the spirit of Paulus Bril's early works. With its pleasant and picturesque presentation of antique monuments, the well balanced and harmonious composition offers a solemn and yet cheerful frame to biblical characters, who are hardly larger than staffage figures. The faithful and exact representation of the Roman ruin of the foreground as well as of the Igel Memorial proves that the master's interest in archaeology did not flag even after several decades. In the brilliant sunshine, the Colosseum and its surroundings painted in delicate, gentle colours appear as a frequently recalled vision. The view is emphasized by the foreground, animated with varied motifs, framed on both sides with darker repoussoirs.

* *Exposition de tableaux de maîtres flamands du XVe au XVIIe siècle.* No. 8. Brussels, 1965. No. 35.

WILLEM VAN NIEULANDT THE YOUNGER

VIEW OF ROME WITH BIBLICAL SCENES (detail)

SEBASTIAN VRANCX
Antwerp, 1573 – Antwerp, 1647

JANUARY

Budapest, Museum of Fine Arts, No. 8242
Oak, 27 × 37 cm
In 1926 it was listed at the XXXIIIrd auction of the Ernst Museum in Budapest (No. 868). For a time it was in the collection of Frigyes Glück; in 1942 it was bequeathed by Fülöp Weiss to the Museum
This picture is from a series representing the months. Another painting of the series, *September*, is also in the Budapest Museum (No. 6519). Vrancx painted the same subject several times and, together with three other representations of months, a picture *January* was listed in 1930 at the auction by R. Lepke in Berlin of the Vierweg Collection of Braunschweig (No. 38). Another version was exhibited by P. de Boer in 1934.*

Even as late as the seventeenth century the pretext of a subject is sometimes found in Netherlandish landscape paintings, and it was thus that Vrancx painted this fine winter townscape as symbolizing January. Compared to earlier pictures of the same subject, this composition is somewhat crowded, there are many figures and many richly varied motifs on a small surface. Thus, the picture evokes animated, busy urban life, instead of the quiet mood of a winter landscape. The frozen river and the row of houses flanking it draw the spectator's eyes inwards, while the moving, teeming figures getting smaller and smaller also serve to intensify the perspective. The diverse and often intersecting shapes of the various motifs set behind one another increase the visual appeal of the picture. Vrancx kept the general effect of the painting attractively muted by his greyish-brownish colours and applied only small areas of stronger colours here and there.

* *De Helsche en de Fluweelen Brueghel*. Amsterdam, 1934. No. 223.

SEBASTIAN VRANCX

JANUARY (detail)

JAN BRUEGHEL THE ELDER
Brussels, 1568 – Antwerp, 1625

THE FALL

Budapest, Museum of Fine Arts, No. 550
Oak, 52 × 83.5 cm
Signed at the bottom left: "BRVEGHEL 16."
This painting belonged to the collection of Prince Kaunitz and from 1821 onwards to the Esterházy Collection.
A replica of the picture is in the Prado, Madrid (No. 1408). There are workshop versions at the Galleria Doria
Pamphili, Rome, in the Castello Sforzesco, Milan, and one used to be at J. Goudstikker in Amsterdam. A copy
signed by Izaak van Oosten is in the Liechtenstein Collection, and another one in the Museum of Toledo

Everything in the world that interested Jan Brueghel as a painter, everything which he
specialized in painting, is included in this composition: the wooded landscape with huge
trees looking out over the hilly country; various birds and animals, flowers painted beautifully,
with virtuoso skill. The picture shows Paradise, where the parents of mankind lived in bliss;
but it hardly differs from other landscapes by Jan Brueghel, since he always depicted nature
in dream-like perfection and beauty. He conveyed the texture of all the details with miraculous
accuracy: the rough bark and rich foliage of the trees, the smoothness of a blade of grass, the
multicoloured plumage of birds—and yet the overall effect of the picture is that of an ideal-
ization. The magnificent colours serve to enhance the supernatural perfection of phenomena,
creatures and objects represented. The bright greens and blues dazzle with an unrealistic
brilliance, particularly where light falls upon them, and appear unnatural. In accordance with
his aspirations to achieve a unified whole, in his late pictures only few colours are used, with
the different shades of green dominating; in the foreground, they are blended with a little
brown, but towards the middle of the picture they grow stronger and clearer, until without
any transition the greens meet a thin, blue streak that indicates a chain of mountains in the
distance, blending into the blue of the sky.

41 JAN BRUEGHEL THE ELDER

THE FALL (detail)

JAN BRUEGHEL THE ELDER

AENEAS IN THE UNDERWORLD WITH THE SIBYL

Budapest, Museum of Fine Arts, No. 551
Copper plate, 26.4 × 36.2 cm
Signed at the bottom left: "[BRVE]GHEL . 160."
From the Esterházy Collection
There is a counterpart or another version of this painting in the Museum of Fine Arts (No. 553). There are also other pictures of the same subjects in the museums in Brussels and Vienna

The subject of the composition refers to the lines in Canto VI of Virgil's *Aeneid*, which describe how Aeneas, arriving with the Sibyl in the Underworld, meets monsters of disease, fear, death, hunger and strife. Contrasting with the paradisiac landscape of the previous picture, here everything is dismal and awe-inspiring; almost bare, dark rocks rise steeply on both banks of the River Styx. In the background the meandering river is illuminated by the white glow of a fire. The sharp, cold white light thrown on groups wandering in the darkness of the near and middle distance is equally eerie, as is the billowing red smoke from the flames behind the cliff. The strong light falling at unexpected points here and there intensifies the already chaotic effect of the composition.

In depicting this bleak, fantastic landscape Jan Brueghel utilized the structure and some motifs of an earlier prototype, the so-called *weltlandschaft* is recalled by the panorama of the river-valley meandering between rocky mountains. In conjuring up an inferno, the painter was influenced by the products of Bosch's imagination. The figures tortured by monsters in the middle of the picture are painted in a particularly attractive style. Indeed, the high painterly qualities of the composition stand out especially in the different groups painted in cold, pale colours, whereas the landscape only serves the purpose of a setting, and of providing the infernal scene with its awe-inspiring atmosphere.

JAN BRUEGHEL THE ELDER

AENEAS IN THE UNDERWORLD WITH THE SIBYL (detail)

44

ABRAHAM GOVAERTS
Antwerp, 1589 – Antwerp, 1626

LANDSCAPE WITH FISHERMEN

Budapest, Museum of Fine Arts, No. 377
Oak, 45.5 × 73.5 cm
This painting came from the Brussels collection of the Archduke Wilhelm Leopold. In 1781 it was transferred from the imperial collection in Vienna to the Castle of Pozsony (Bratislava) and from there to the Buda residence of the Treasurer of Hungary. In 1848 it passed into the possession of the Hungarian National Museum and in 1896 to the Museum of Fine Arts

The composition and motifs—the avenue of trees on the right leading into the depth, and on the left, a view of a distant landscape—correspond with Coninxloo's popular type of landscapes. Although the details are realistic, the painting does not represent a real scene, but an idealistic dream world irradiated by a romantic love of nature. This very emotion, and the intensification of such elements as imbue the picture with feeling, make Govaerts's works different from the paintings of artists of the previous generation, as for example of Jan Brueghel, who had none the less influenced him greatly. The rich foliage, the luxuriant vegetation display this influence; so do the bright greens and blues, and the types of the staffage figures. However, with Govaerts the vegetation is even more dense and exuberant, softer and more pictorial in its effect. Further a powerful sense of movement pervades the whole composition, as well as the details. The whimsically jagged silhouettes of the foliage, the dark clouds in the sky and the sharp light piercing them here and there, the surface of water rippled by the wind, the brisk and busy figures, all contribute to creating an effect of animation and variety.

ABRAHAM GOVAERTS

LANDSCAPE WITH FISHERMEN (detail)

ABRAHAM GOVAERTS

Mountain Landscape with River

Budapest, Museum of Fine Arts, No. 379
Oak, 45.5 × 73.5 cm
From the Brussels collection of the Archduke Wilhelm Leopold, it was transferred from the Vienna imperial collection in 1781 to the Castle of Pozsony (Bratislava) and from there to the Buda residence of the Treasurer of Hungary. In 1848 it passed into the possession of the Hungarian National Museum, and in 1896 to the Museum of Fine Arts

This forms a companion-piece of the previous picture, but it is even more lyrical in mood and more pictorial in treatment. The spacious, open river-valley seen from a higher point, and the part of the dense woods on the left, create an exquisite contrast both from an emotional and from a pictorial point of view. The composition and its separate motifs and the dead, dry trees with high clumps of grass in the foreground recall Coninxloo and Jan Brueghel, but depicted in a more pictorial manner, and with stronger lyricism. Indeed, the dead tree in the foreground is a motif frequently found in Jan Brueghel's paintings but with him the bare branches outlined against the light sky are never emphasized so strongly and do not intensify the romantic mood of the whole composition to the same extent. Painted in shades of deep blue, the dream-like panorama of the river-valley, shrouded in a delicate mist, blends the separate details in a homogeneous, picturesque whole, while the remote mountains beyond the river, with their outlines softening gradually, disappear in the distance.

47 ABRAHAM GOVAERTS

Mountain Landscape with River (detail)

ROELANDT SAVERY
Kortrijk, 1576 – Utrecht, 1639

ROCKY LANDSCAPE

Budapest, Museum of Fine Arts, No. 5559
Canvas, 117 × 157.5 cm
Signed at the bottom centre: "R SAVERY"
Donated by Moritz Heim, Vienna, in 1920

Compared to other compositions by Savery, mostly animated, romantic and fairy-tale like, this picture is more epic, meditative. It reveals the extent to which the painter must have been moved by the majestic world of the mountains, and by their deep silence. As in most of his pictures, here too Savery arranged the motifs of the alpine landscape in Coninxloo's manner of composition. On both sides of the foreground he placed trees painted in great detail and he crowded the various motifs into the middle: sheer cliffs, partially obscuring the view, a tumbling mountain stream and a variety of tall trees. He is more faithful to nature here than in his other works; the objectivity of his observation overcame his penchant for decorativeness. Similarly, the light is more even, there are no sharp contrasts of light and shade; thus the composition is imbued with a joyous serenity. The colours are somewhat muted: the foreground is greyish-brown, enlivened only by the brighter green of the trees outlined against the blue shades of the background.